Imagination with Words

HERON
BOOKS
K-12 CURRICULUM

At Heron Books, we think learning should be engaging and fun. It should be hands-on and it should allow students to move at their own pace.

For this purpose, we have created an accompanying learning guide to help the student progress through this book, chapter by chapter, with increasing confidence, interest and independence.

Get your free learning guide at
heronbooks.com/learningguides.

For a final exam, email
teacherresources@heronbooks.com.

We would love to hear from you!
Email us at *feedback@heronbooks.com.*

Published by
Heron Books, Inc.
20950 SW Rock Creek Road
Sheridan, OR 97378

heronbooks.com

———————

Special thanks to all the teachers and students who
provided feedback instrumental to this edition.

———————

In This Book

CHAPTER 1
What Writers Do

What Writers Do

Writers like to tell us things. They like to tell us how to do things. They like to tell us what things look like, how they feel, how they smell, what color they are.

They like to tell us about places. Are they beautiful or ugly? Do they seem scary or safe?

They like to tell us about people. What do they look like? Are they grumpy? Are they friendly? Are they happy or sad? Do they look like they just got out of bed?

Writers do a lot of describing. You have done a lot of this in your own writing. So you may have learned that a writer can describe things in different ways. He or she can use writing that is plain or writing that is more imaginative.

Here, for example, is a plain sentence. *The red, white and blue kite went up into the sky.*

Here is a sentence that says this in a more imaginative way. *The red, white and blue kite sailed up, then hung in the sky like a bright American flag.*

This helps you use your imagination to picture the kite.

This book is about both kinds of writing.

Most especially it is about the imaginative kind.

Knowing about imaginative writing can be useful to you as a writer, and also as a reader.

You can learn how to describe things in imaginative ways.

And you can enjoy the imaginative writing others have created for you to read.

CHAPTER 2

Plain Writing for Information

Plain Writing for Information

2

First, let's talk a little about plain writing.

Sometimes we read because we want information. We might want to know where something is, how it works, or how to do something.

Actually, we read this kind of writing a lot. The directions for a workbook page, for example, tell you how to do it. A pudding recipe tells you the exact steps for making a yummy dessert. A spelling rule tells you how to spell a certain kind of word.

Sometimes this kind of writing gives us facts. A book about mammals might say this.

> *Mammals have hair or fur. They don't lay eggs. They give birth to live babies, and mothers feed their babies milk.*

This tells you facts—things that are true.

Directions and facts must be easy to understand, so this kind of writing is perfect for that because it's simple and clear. It tells you exactly what you want to know. There's nothing fancy about it.

Here's an example from the book *Air.*

> "Wind is moving air. Wind can bend trees. Wind can make flags fly. Sailboats move because of wind. Wind helps kites fly."

See how plain and simple the writing is? And how easy it is to get the idea?

Here's another example from *An Octopus is Amazing.*

> "Every octopus lives alone. Its den is small, just big enough to hold the octopus. An octopus can squeeze into a small space because it has no backbone. In fact, it has no bones at all."

In both of these, the plain, clear writing makes the information easy to understand.

CHAPTER 3

Plain Writing That Describes Things

Plain Writing That Describes Things

3

When they're writing, writers often describe things. They give you a clear picture of something by saying exactly how it is. A writer might describe a tree like this. *It's tall, with lots of curvy branches, and big purplish leaves.*

Here's an example from the book *Tornado.*

> "The storm cellar was dim and cool. It smelled of potatoes and pickles. My mother kept sacks of root vegetables here along with boxes of eggs and jars of tomatoes."

It tells you clearly and exactly what the cellar is like and what's there. Can't you kind of feel the dark, cool cellar, smell the potatoes and see the boxes of eggs?

Here's another example from the book *Look at Lucy!*

> "Lucy wasn't the kind of dog who liked to sit. She was the kind of dog who liked to run and jump. She liked to run so much that a few weeks ago she had run away."

The simple clear writing makes it easy to get a good picture of Lucy in your mind, and you know just what she is like.

CHAPTER 4

Another Way to Describe Things

Another Way to Describe Things

Sometimes a writer likes to describe things in a more imaginative way.

Here's an example from the book *More Stories Julian Tells*.

> "The bridge was long and silver and sparkled in the sun.
> It was so big that it looked like giants must have made it,
> that human beings never could have."

Instead of simply saying "the bridge was huge," the writer has come up with an interesting, imaginative way to describe it. It's fun to use your imagination to picture a bridge so big it looks like giants built it.

Look at this from *The Stories Julian Tells*.

> "My father is a big man with wild black hair and when he
> laughs, the sun laughs in the windowpanes."

In other words, when Julian's dad laughs, everything is brighter, as though the sun is laughing too.

Writing like this gives a lively picture. It's creative. It's fun for a writer to write and a reader to read.

CHAPTER 5

More About
Imaginative Writing

More About
Imaginative Writing

5

As you can see, when we talk about imaginative writing, we don't just mean that the writer imagined stories or the people in them, or that he or she thought up a bunch of wild things to write about. Of course, that would be writing with imagination. But here we are talking about putting words together in imaginative ways to describe what something looks, feels or even smells, tastes or sounds like.

In *The Stories Julian Tells,* Julian and his brother Huey take bite after bite of the fresh lemon pudding their father has made especially for their mother. What does it look like after that? According to Julian "it looked like craters on the moon." That's an imaginative and interesting way to describe it!

Later, Julian and Huey's father finds them hiding from him under the bed. "There was his face, and his eyes like black lightning." What picture do you get in your mind of Julian's dad?

Here's an example from a book called *The Adventures of Buster Bear.*

> "Buster Bear listened to a merry, low, silvery laugh that never stopped but went on and on, until he just felt as if he must laugh too. It was the voice of the Laughing Brook."

Isn't this a lively, playful way to describe a bubbling brook? Maybe you could think of another imaginative way to describe it yourself.

CHAPTER 6

Why Writers Use Imaginative Writing

Why Writers Use Imaginative Writing 6

If you wanted to describe a nice spring day, you could do it plainly. You might name the color of the sky, say what flowers are there, explain how hot or cold it is, tell about the smell of the air and so on. For example,

> *It's a lovely spring day. The sky is blue, the daffodils are yellow, the air is warm, and everything smells clean and fresh.*

That gives you a good idea of that day. But you could also describe it imaginatively. You might say

> *This spring day is so beautiful it makes even grumpy old men want to jump for joy.*

Imaginative writing makes stories livelier and more interesting. As writers, we get to create interesting lively pictures for readers. As readers, we get to use our own imaginations to really see and feel what is going on in a story.

When a writer is very good at writing imaginatively, a story can become so real that we almost feel like it is happening to us.

CHAPTER 7

Understanding Imaginative Writing

Understanding Imaginative Writing

7

As you read, you will come across sentences that are written with a lot of imagination. The main thing you need to know about these is that you can't always read them the way you read plain writing that is giving you information. Sometimes you need to use your own imagination to get what is meant.

In imaginative writing, words are not just put together with all of their plain, ordinary meanings. Instead, the writer puts them together in an imaginative way to describe something that has happened or what something feels like, looks like or sounds like. The writer chooses his or her words so that when you read them using your own imagination, you can get a picture of what happened or feel the feeling yourself.

WHAT YOU CAN DO

When you read a piece of imaginative writing, you might have to pause for a moment and work out what the writer is saying. Here's a sentence from the story "Anna Hibiscus Sells Oranges."

"The big, bright smile fell off Anna Hibiscus's face."

Did Anna's smile *actually* fall off and hit the ground? Well, let's see. What picture does this sentence give you? If we look imaginatively, it seems that her face suddenly went from happy and smiling to definitely not smiling and, perhaps, unhappy. It's said in an imaginative way that gives us a lively picture of what is happening with Anna.

Here's another example, from the book *The Adventures of Buster Bear.* This one might seem a little trickier.

> "Buster Bear yawned as he lay on his comfortable bed of leaves and watched the first early morning sunbeams creeping through the Green Forest to chase out the Black Shadows."

Now, pretend this piece of imaginative writing didn't make sense to you. What could you do?

First, you would want to make sure you understand the words the writer is using. Suppose you decide you don't really know what "creeping" means, so you look for it in your dictionary. Oh! One meaning is "moving slowly." But sunbeams don't actually move like that. Also, they can't chase shadows. So what does the whole thing mean?

This would be a good time to try using your imagination to see what feeling or picture the writer is giving you. This piece of imaginative writing seems to describe morning sunbeams slowly moving deeper and deeper into the forest (as the sun goes up higher and higher). This brightens the forest and makes the shady spots (shadows) disappear. The writer says the sunbeams "chase out the Black Shadows."

This piece of imaginative writing "paints" (an imaginative way of saying "makes") a picture of morning sunbeams slowly bringing light into the forest. You can't understand it by just stringing the meanings of the words together, one by one. This won't give you the picture. In imaginative writing, you have to understand the words, and use your imagination to get an idea of the picture the writer is painting.

CHAPTER 8

Now What?

Now What?

Now you understand a little more about two different kinds of writing.

Some writing is plain and clear, and some is more imaginative.

Both kinds are interesting, and fun to create. You can use both when you write.

And when you come across some imaginative writing as you read, it will be easier to understand and enjoy!

The last chapter of this book gives examples of imaginative writing for you to have fun imagining what the writer is describing.

CHAPTER 9

Examples of Imaginative Writing

Examples of Imaginative Writing

1. Marven came upon a frozen lake covered with snow, which lay in a circle of tall trees like a bowl of sugar. (*Marven of the Great North Woods*)

2. Billy Mink was feeling very good indeed. The sun was warm, little white cloud ships were sailing across the blue sky and their shadows were sailing across the Green Meadows. (*Old Mother West Wind*)

3. It was a hot summer day. As Huey, Gloria and I walked, the sun shined up at us from the sidewalks. Even the shadows on the street were hot as blankets. (*More Stories Julian Tells*)

4. "That kind of man," I said. My words came out all white and thin, like a little skinny piece of spaghetti. (*Julian's Glorious Summer*)

5. It did feel good to tell the truth. Once I began to tell the truth, it seemed like it almost had a taste, like some really delicious food to chew on, that I wanted to have more and more of in my mouth. (*Julian's Glorious Summer*)

6. Gramercy Park was a beautiful place. There were flowers of all different colors; it was as if an over-ripe rainbow had burst and scattered its seeds over Gramercy Park. The lawn was clipped as neat and nice as a new haircut. (*Harry Kitten and Tucker Mouse*)

7. "Tucker Mouse." It sounded quite original. Not ordinary, like Tom, or Bill, or Joe. "Tucker Mouse" he shouted! "That's me." The name tasted more sweet and more strong in his mouth than even a raspberry tart. *(Harry Kitten and Tucker Mouse)*

8. When my father is angry, me and my little brother, Huey, shiver to the bottom of our shoes. *(The Stories Julian Tells)*

9. It's a wonderful pudding, with waves on top like the ocean. *(The Stories Julian Tells)*

10. Jean Louis opened one eye. It glittered like a blue star beneath his thick black eyebrow. *(Marven of the Great North Woods)*

11. "My, what a neat little desk you have there." Roger bent down and stuck his head right inside Marsha's desk like he was checking pies in an oven. *(Good Grief…Third Grade)*

12. If my father has customers in his shop, he always introduces us as if we were important guests. We get to shake hands and feel like visiting mayors. *(More Stories Julian Tells)*

13. A teacher waited at the door to inspect us. She was a horrible woman. She had a long sharp nose like a knife and her hair was pulled back so tightly that it looked like it was painted onto her head. *(The Year of the Dog)*

14. Marsha slammed down her desktop so hard, Roger's fingertips almost snapped off. He started hopping up and down like he was on a hot black skillet. *(Good Grief…Third Grade)*

15. My father smiled again, like a cobra. *(More Stories Julian Tells)*

16. He was so short his chin would have been under water in the shallow end of any swimming-pool in the world. (*Fantastic Mr. Fox*)

17. Melody and Felix handed me a big wooden crate overflowing with oranges. There were a lot of oranges. They kept jumping out of the crate, like rabbits trying to escape. (*The Year of the Dog*)

18. He threw his hands high in the air and raised his eyes to the sky, as if he wanted to make sure heaven was listening. (*Julian's Glorious Summer*)

19. Gloria's smile came out sudden and shining, like a rainbow after a storm. (*Julian's Glorious Summer*)

20. I tried to sound braver than ever, like a spaceboy who had to be left behind on an asteroid. (*Julian's Glorious Summer*)

21. Aunt Alice rushed over like a typhoon and hurried me out of the chair. (*The Year of the Dog*)

22. At night, when Laura lay awake in bed, she listened and could not hear anything at all but the sound of the trees whispering together. (*Little House in the Big Woods*)

23. Her eyes were pleading and full of tears. They reminded me of a baby rabbit caught in a trap. (*The Year of the Dog*)

24. I felt the way I feel during a horror movie when I don't like how the story is going and I want to leave. (*Julian's Glorious Summer*)

25. The cattails kept their feet cool in the edge of the Laughing Brook. (*Old Mother West Wind*)

26. Snip! Snip! I saw my hair flutter down to the ground like a dying moth. *(The Year of the Dog)*

27. Bugs Meany had one dream in life. It was to get even with Encyclopedia. Bugs hated being outsmarted all the time. He dreamed of punching Encyclopedia in the mouth so hard that his eyes would be looking for his teeth. *(Encyclopedia Brown Lends a Hand)*

28. "HEL-lo, Julian!" my dad said in a super-friendly voice. Usually that voice means trouble. I checked my dad's eyes. Sure enough, little red and blue flames were leaping in them, like a furnace that would melt steel. *(Julian's Glorious Summer)*

29. I was riding my bike for the first time. I kept pedaling. It started to seem like I was standing still. Trees and houses floated by me, like green ships and like white ones. *(Julian's Glorious Summer)*

30. My head jerked up. My eyes jumped open like electric-eye doors. *(Julian's Glorious Summer)*

31. Sometimes my father notices too much. Then he gets yellow lights shining in his eyes, asking you to tell the whole truth. *(More Stories Julian Tells)*

32. The new girl had straight black hair that shone in the sun, just like Ginny's. She had bangs cut straight across, just like Ginny's. Another Chinese girl. Ginny's heart did a little dance. *(The Jade Dragon)*

33. Thick trees climbed the distant mountainsides like rows of tall green soldiers marching toward the top. *(Bread-and-Butter Indian)*

34. Flory was at home in the dark. She had great sharp eyes that sparkled like blackberries under dew. *(The Night Fairy)*

35. My dad gave me an extra-big steel-bending smile. *(Julian's Glorious Summer)*

36. We went out of the air-conditioned restaurant and the heat wrapped around us again. *(Julian, Secret Agent)*

37. The sun was bright. It poured melted gold from the blue sky over the soft grass meadows of the valley. *(Bread-and-Butter Indian)*

38. Suddenly my dad bent his knees and slid down as fast as if he was sliding down an invisible firehouse pole, until he was sitting on his knees and looking up into my face. *(Julian's Glorious Summer)*

39. In Anna's journal, the words walk across the page like bird prints in the mud. But it's hard for me to find things to write about. *(Caleb's Story)*

40. There was the sudden sound of hail, like stones tossed against the barn. We stared out the window, watching the ice marbles bounce on the ground. *(Sarah, Plain and Tall)*